a little book of
friendship

Especially for _____

Beatrix Potter Collection™

The C.R. Gibson Company
Norwalk, Connecticut

A friend is a present you
give yourself.

Robert Louis Stevenson

True friendship multiplies the good in life and divides its evils. Strive to have friends, for life without friends is like life on a desert island....
To find one real friend in a lifetime is good fortune; to keep him, a blessing.

Baltasar Gracian

Don't walk in front of me —
   I may not follow.
Don't walk behind me —
   I may not lead.
Walk beside me —
   and just be my friend.

Four things are specially
the property of friendship:
love and affection, security
and joy.

Aelred of Rievaulx

Every house where love abides
   And friendship is a guest,
Is surely home, and home,
            sweet home
For there the heart
         can rest.

Henry van Dyke

DAILY CREED

Let me be a little kinder,
Let me be a little blinder
To the faults of those about me,
Let me praise a little more.

Let me be, when I am weary,
Just a little bit more cheery;
Let me serve a little better
The God we would adore.

Let me be a little meeker
With the brother who is weaker;
Let me strive a little harder
To be all that I should be.

Let me be more understanding,
And a little less demanding,
Let me be the sort of friend
That you have always been to me.

John Grey

The friends of my friends
are my friends.

French Proverb

Friendship is born at the
moment when one person
says to another "What!
You too? I thought that
no one but myself..."

C. S. Lewis

A friend may well be reckoned
the masterpiece of Nature.

Ralph Waldo Emerson

Friendship is a growing thing.
It keeps on getting bigger and
stronger the longer you
share it.

Dean Walley

Friendship? Yes, please.

Charles Dickens

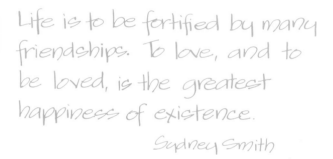

Life is to be fortified by many
friendships. To love, and to
be loved, is the greatest
happiness of existence.

Sydney Smith